THE BEAUTY OF
NAVAJO JEWELRY

By Theda Bassman

Photography by Gene Balzer

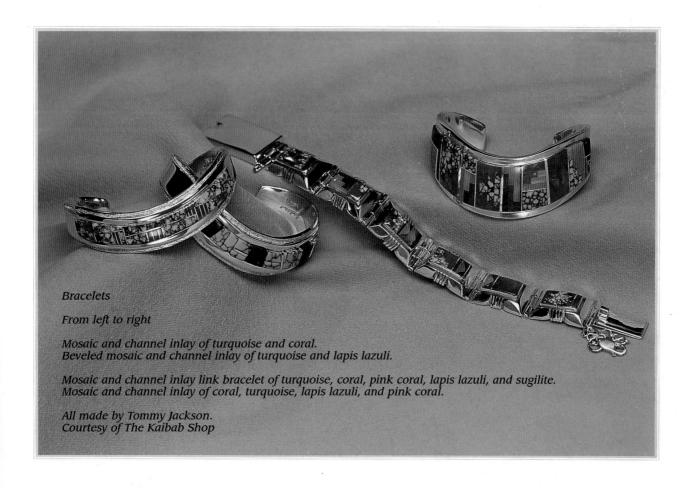

Bracelets

From left to right

Mosaic and channel inlay of turquoise and coral.
Beveled mosaic and channel inlay of turquoise and lapis lazuli.

Mosaic and channel inlay link bracelet of turquoise, coral, pink coral, lapis lazuli, and sugilite.
Mosaic and channel inlay of coral, turquoise, lapis lazuli, and pink coral.

All made by Tommy Jackson.
Courtesy of The Kaibab Shop

Front Cover Photo

Old style squash blossom necklace with stamped silver and twelve Chinese turquoise stones with earrings to match made by Ray Tracey.
Courtesy of the artist.

Library of Congress Catalog Card Number 97-070356

Publisher's Cataloging in Publication
(Prepared by Quality Books Inc.)

Bassman, Theda
The beauty of Navajo jewelry / Theda Bassman ; photography by Gene Balzer.
p. cm.
Includes bibliographical references and index.
ISBN 1-885772-02-5

1. Navajo Indians-Jewelry. 2. Navajo silverwork. I. Balzer, Gene. II. Title.
E99.N3B377 1997   739.27'089'972
QBI97-40216

Kiva Publishing, Inc.
102 East Water Street
Santa Fe, NM 87501

Designed by Steve Marsh
Printed in Hong Kong
9 8 7 6 5 4 3 2 1

DEDICATION

I dedicate this book to my good friends, Nancie and Sterling Mahan.
Their confidence in me from the beginning has been a great source of joy.
Their help and encouragement have been given with charm and good humor.

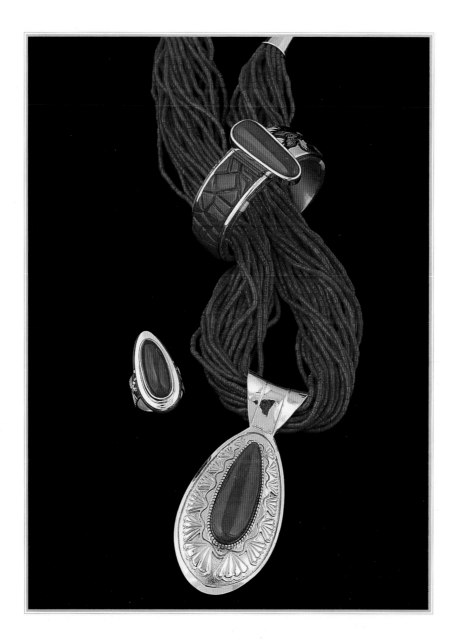

*Twenty-seven strand coral heishe necklace with pendant of 14-karat
gold, overlay and repoussé work, and 14-karat gold beads and cones.*

*Silver bracelet of beveled and mosaic inlay is of oxblood coral and
Kingman turquoise on one end and an eagle on the other. The eagle is
of flat mosaic inlay of white mother-of-pearl and penn shell.*

*The shank of the ring is silver stampwork. The sides next to the oxblood
coral stone are mosaic inlay.*

*All made by Jake Livingston.
Courtesy of the artist.*

ACKNOWLEDGMENTS

My thanks to the following people who so graciously permitted their jewelry to be photographed:

> Jake Livingston
>
> Perry Shorty
>
> Ray Tracey
>
> Raymond Yazzie

And all of the private collectors who wish to remain anonymous.

Additional thanks to the galleries and their staffs who provided me with jewelry and help:

> R. B. Burnham & Co. Trading Post, Sanders, Arizona
>
> Gallup Indian Plaza, Gallup, New Mexico
>
> Garland's Indian Jewelry, Sedona, Arizona
>
> The Kaibab Shop, Tucson, Arizona
>
> Many Hands Gallery, Sedona, Arizona
>
> McGee's Beyond Native Tradition, Holbrook, Arizona
>
> Tanner's Indian Arts, Gallup, New Mexico

A special thanks to Lynn Valeruz, who spent many hours with me identifying stones and silver work.

My thanks to my wonderful photographer, Gene Balzer, who manages to capture with his camera all that I want to say.

Lastly, my heartfelt thanks to my husband, Michael, who is the soul of patience in helping me with proofreading, over and over again, and for his suggestions after reading all that I had written.

NOTE ON THE TEXT
All jewelry is sterling silver unless otherwise noted. All gold jewelry is 14-karat gold unless otherwise noted. All coral is Mediterranean coral.

INTRODUCTION

The Navajos refer to themselves as Diné, which means *the people*. They are the largest Native American tribe in the United States, consisting of more than 200,000 members. Their reservation encompasses sixteen million acres in Arizona, New Mexico, and Utah.

The Navajos were driven from their land and incarcerated by the United States Government from 1864-1868 in Fort Sumner, New Mexico. When they were released, they returned to their homeland. It was at this time they learned the art of silversmithing from the neighboring Mexicans. Nakai Tsosi, a Mexican blacksmith, developed silversmithing skills and taught them to a Navajo, Atsidi Sani.

As new tools and ideas developed, so did the art of silversmithing. At first, silver coins were melted and used in making jewelry. In 1890, when the United States Government banned this procedure, the silversmiths began to use Mexican pesos, which were supplied by trader John Lawrence Hubbell at Ganado, Arizona. Shortly afterwards, these finished products were banned for export, and then the traders began to supply silver to the Navajos.

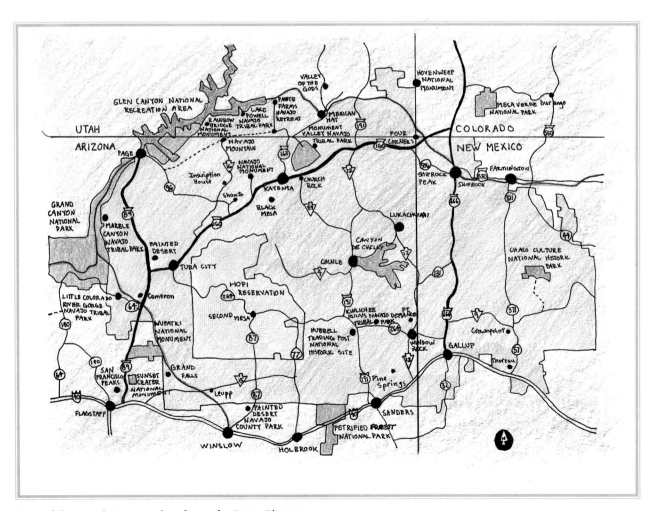

Map of the Navajo Reservation drawn by Doug Pierson

The Navajos greatly admired the silverwork of the early Spaniards, who loved personal adornment that was lavishly decorated with silver. One example is the *naja*, a crescent-shaped pendant appearing on the bridles of the Spanish horses, originally used by the Moors of North Africa, and eventually copied by the Navajos. Today, the *naja* is still used as a pendant on squash blossom necklaces and other jewelry. Another ancient design adopted by the Navajos is the squash blossom. As early as 100 B.C. this design, which is really of pomegranate blossoms, was used in Persia. Popularized by the Navajos, it is known today as "squash blossom."

Another decorative element previously used in far-flung cultures is turquoise. Sparingly incorporated in silversmithing in ancient Egypt, Persia, China, and Tibet, turquoise was first set in silver by Navajo silversmiths about 1880, and by 1890 it was used in abundance. The traders were supplying tools for the silversmiths at about the same time, and so the jewelry became more refined, especially with the stamps which were used to press the designs into the silver.

By the 1920's and 1930's, turquoise was extensively used by the Navajo silversmiths. During the 1920's the traders also supplied them with wire, sheet silver, and coral. Thus began the tradition, carried out to this day, of traders supplying stones and silver to the Navajos for making jewelry. In return, the Navajos sold the finished pieces to the traders. The traders had great influence on the style of the jewelry, and the silversmiths were free in discussing their ideas with the traders. This exchange of ideas resulted in new ideas and new designs. The Navajos also borrowed ideas from other tribes and incorporated them into a uniquely Navajo pattern and design. New techniques were developed through the creativity of the craftsmen. In the technique of sand or tufa casting, the design was carved into a piece of sandstone or tufa. A second piece which was left uncarved was tied tightly to the first piece, and melted silver was poured into the mold. When cooled, the silver piece was filed and polished. This technique is used today. In another technique, punches are used to stamp designs on the silver. The punch is hit by a hammer until the design is impressed in the silver or leather.

One of the hallmarks of Navajo jewelry is the extensive use of turquoise. The sacred stone of all Native American people of the Southwest, turquoise has a spiritual healing significance. It is said to keep the person who is wearing it from harm. Turquoise comes in many shades of blues and greens and has a hardness of 5-6 in the Mohs scale of hardness used in mineralogy. Navajo men as well as the women adorn themselves with jewelry, bracelets being the more popular item. The men and women will often be buried with their jewelry.

In the 1920's and 1930's, very large and heavy turquoise stones were used in the jewelry, which made it more valuable when it was placed in pawn. Pawn is part of the culture of the Navajos. They would rather put their wealth into jewelry than money, for the item can be pawned over and over again. It can be borrowed against or traded for food and clothing. Some of the older Navajos pawn their jewelry to keep it safe. During ceremonial gatherings, the Navajos bedeck themselves lavishly in turquoise jewelry. This is one of the times they take their jewelry out of pawn, only to put it back again after the ceremony.

Pawn room of R. B. Burnham & Co. Trading Post

Trader Bruce Burnham of Sanders, Arizona, says that he likes to get pawn pieces back to the families as soon as possible. After six months, he sends out a notice saying that the pawn piece should be picked up in a month according to their agreement. He waits two more weeks and then sends a certified letter. If the piece is not called for, it then becomes part of his inventory. The 2% a month interest stops, and the piece becomes "dead pawn" and can be sold. If the owner comes in after the allotted time, Burnham will allow the piece to be redeemed if he still has it. He states that he doesn't want to sell a piece that has been in a Navajo family for years, since it is important to him to maintain a friendly and personal relationship with the family. In the case of an heirloom piece, he will hold it for as long as fifteen years. Other items of value, such as chainsaws, televisions and VCR's, and saddles and blankets are also pawned. However, 90% of the pawn is jewelry, and about 10% of that ends up as dead pawn.

Most Navajo jewelry is still made in the traditional and classic way. However, some artists are changing styles, forging new ideas and techniques, using inlay of precious and semiprecious stones, channel work, mosaic inlay, and overlay. In addition, the sophisticated use of gold and diamonds has transformed jewelry making from craft to art. The versatility and artistry of Navajo jewelry knows no bounds.

In the Making

Unfinished jewelry

From left to right

Row 1
Bracelet by Raymond Yazzie. Bracelet by Jake Livingston. Stones to be set will be lapis lazuli, red and pink coral, and Kingman turquoise.

Row 2
Two gold rings by Raymond Yazzie. Stones to be set will be coral, lapis lazuli, and turquoise.

Concha belt with traditional Navajo stamp and repoussé work with stones of McGinnis turquoise. Made by Perry Shorty.

Loose stones are Bisbee, Kingman, and McGinnis turquoise and red coral. Courtesy of the artists.

In the Making

Overlay and repoussé silver box being made will have a catch and lid. The red coral and Nevada Blue turquoise stones will be incorporated into the lid.

The two finished necklaces resting in the box are of traditional Navajo stampwork with red coral and Nevada Blue turquoise.

All of the above are made by Jake Livingston.

The finished box with silver repoussé work has a Chinese Mountain turquoise stone and forty-two silver dangles on the front and sides, giving the box an elegant and antique look.
Made by Perry Shorty.

Courtesy of the artists.

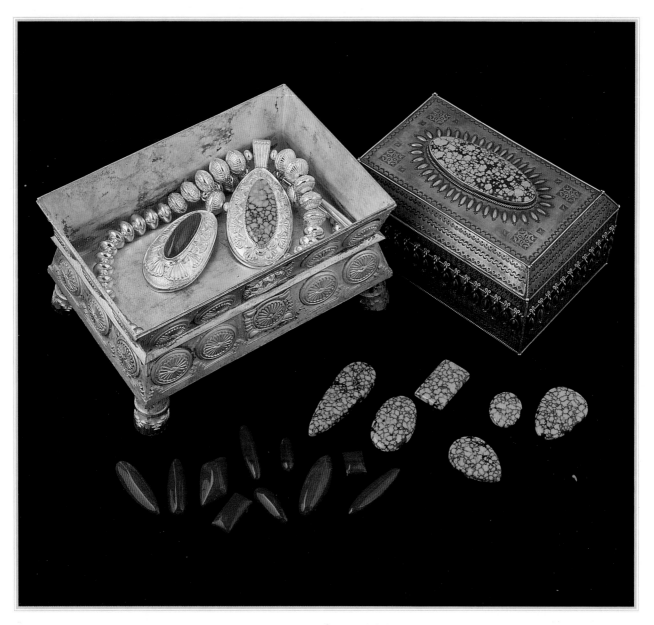

Clockwise from silver stamped belt buckle.

All bracelets.

Three row with thirty-three Arizona turquoise stones.

Cluster with forty-five Cerrillos turquoise stones.

Five row with eighty-eight Lone Mountain turquoise stones.

Seven #8 turquoise stones.

Seven Cerrillos turquoise stones.

Center bracelet with traditional Navajo stamp and repoussé work.

All from the 1920's. Artists unknown.

Courtesy of Tanner's Indian Arts.

From Years Past

Necklace on left with stamped silver beads.

Bracelets from top to bottom.

Row 1
Cluster bracelet with #8 Nevada turquoise.

Bracelet with stampwork and Lone Mountain turquoise.

Bracelet with stamp and repoussé work and a cluster of Lone Mountain turquoise.

Three-stone bracelet with Blue Gem turquoise.

Row 2
Bracelet with stampwork and silver balls and seven stones of Persian turquoise.

Cast bracelet.

Squash blossom necklace.

All from the 1940's.
Artists unknown.

Courtesy of Tanner's Indian Arts.

From Years Past

Necklace, bracelet, and ring with twisted silver rope and stampwork. Contour cut Morenci turquoise.

Made in the 1950's. Artist unknown.

Courtesy of Tanner's Indian Arts.

Variation of a squash blossom necklace of shadow box design, silver beads, and nugget cut Lone Mountain turquoise with matching bracelet, earrings, and ring.

Made in the 1960's by Charles Chee Long.

Courtesy of Tanner's Indian Arts.

From Years Past

Necklace with silver beads made by Lee A. Yazzie. Coral stone set in a cast ornament made by Sam Begay.

From left to right

Cast bracelet with a coral stone made by Evelyn Anderson.

Bracelet with four coral stones made by Joe Yazzie.

Two cast bracelets with coral stones made by Evelyn Anderson.

Ring with a coral stone made by Ed Shirley.

All made in the 1970's.

Courtesy of Tanner's Indian Arts.

From Years Past

From left to right

Squash blossom necklace with square domed beads and a cast naja made by Della and Francis James.

Necklace of fluted chiseled beads made by Minnie Porter.

Necklace of graduated stamped beads made by Minnie Porter.

Squash blossom necklace with stamens emerging from the blossoms made by Della and Francis James.

All made in the 1960's.

Courtesy of Tanner's Indian Arts.

From Years Past

Necklace, earrings, bracelet, and ring with stampwork and Chinese Mountain turquoise made in 1978 by Steve Yellowhorse.

Courtesy of Gallup Indian Plaza.

From Years Past

Squash blossom necklace with fifteen coral stones and silver cast naja with earrings to match.

Silver cast bracelet with four coral stones. This bracelet won First Prize at the New Mexico State Fair in Albuquerque, New Mexico in 1979.

Ring with one coral stone.

All made in the 1970's by Della and Francis James.

Courtesy of Tanner's Indian Arts.

Necklaces

From left to right

Fluted silver beads with hammered and stamped Yei-bi-chai masks. Made by Kee Joe Benally.

Fluted and cone beads with a Bisbee turquoise dangle. Made by Charles Chee Long.

Fluted and cone beads with silver cast pendant and Persian turquoise stone made by Della and Francis James.

All made in the 1970's.

Courtesy of Tanner's Indian Arts.

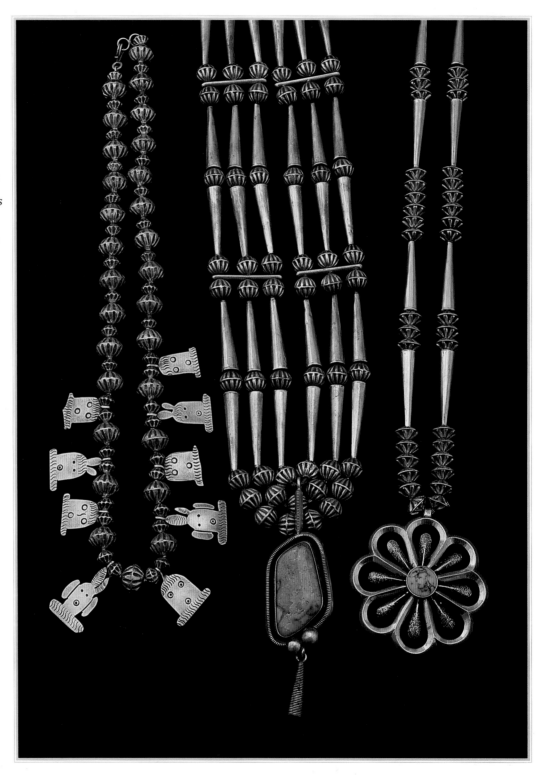

Bracelets

From left to right

Row 1

Inlaid with turquoise, lapis lazuli, salmon, angel and oxblood coral, made by Boyd Tsosie.

Channel and mosaic inlay with sugilite, lapis lazuli, angel coral and turquoise. Stones were set by Clayton Panteah (Zuni) and the silverwork is by James Nez . This bracelet won First Prize at the Gallup Inter-Tribal Indian Ceremonial in Gallup, New Mexico in 1989.

Beveled salmon coral inlaid with gold channel and dot made by Raymond Yazzie. Silver with gold overlay and inlay of lapis lazuli, dolomite, malachite, spiny oyster shell, angel and oxblood coral, and turquoise. Made by Jesse Monongye.

Channel and mosaic inlay with lapis lazuli, turquoise, sugilite, and angel and oxblood coral made by Gibson Nez.

Channel and mosaic turquoise inlay by Norton Becenti and silverwork by Calvin Begay.

Row 2

Beveled oxblood coral, lapis lazuli, Australian opal, and turquoise with gold inlay made by Raymond Yazzie. Channel and mosaic inlay with dolomite, fossilized ivory, and lapis lazuli made by Gibson Nez.

Mosaic inlay of a female Yei figure with jet, turquoise, angel and oxblood coral, white mother-of-pearl, and sugilite made by Jim Harrison.

Beveled inlay of angel and oxblood coral, lapis lazuli, gold, sugilite, turquoise, and textured silver made by Raymond Yazzie.

Mosaic inlay with angel and oxblood coral, lapis lazuli, sugilite, jet, malachite and turquoise made by Boyd Tsosie.

Courtesy of Garland's Indian Jewelry.

Link Bracelets

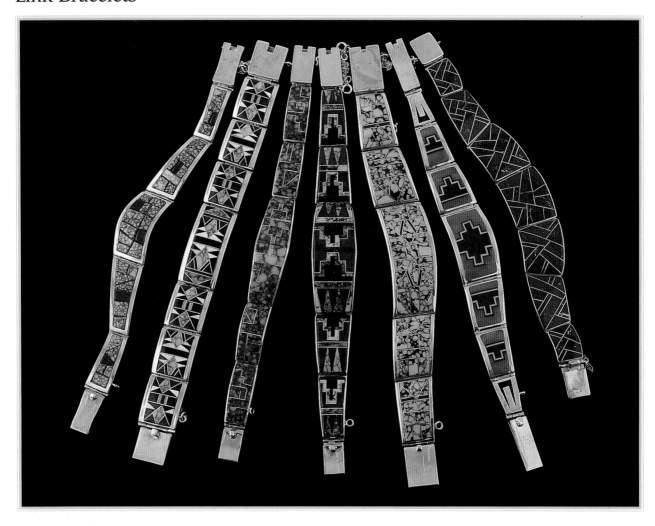

From left to right

Beveled mosaic inlay of turquoise and oxblood coral. Stones were set by Jasper John with silverwork by Rick Tolino.

Channel and mosaic inlay of oxblood coral, turquoise, lapis lazuli, dolomite, jet, and sugilite. Stones were set by Gloria Livingston with silverwork by Rick Tolino.

Turquoise channel and mosaic inlay. Stones were set by Norton Becenti with silverwork by Rick Tolino.

Channel and mosaic inlay with turquoise, lapis lazuli, and sugilite. Stones were set by Norton Becenti with silverwork by Rick Tolino.

Channel inlay with turquoise and lapis lazuli. Stones were set by Zora Joe with silverwork by Rick Tolino.

Mosaic inlay with angel coral, sugilite, and turquoise. Stones were set by Wilbert Muskett, Jr. with silverwork by Julian Arviso.

Channel inlay with sugilite and oxblood coral. Stones were set by Rose Ann Long with silverwork by Irene Kee.

Courtesy of Garland's Indian Jewelry.

Bracelets

From left to right

Row 1
Overlay with sugilite and turquoise made by Cecilia Yazzie.

Stampwork with a Lander Blue turquoise stone made by Dan Jackson.

Stampwork with a Blue Diamond turquoise stone made by Jefferson Abeita.

Row 2
Stampwork and overlay of Flute Players with one turquoise stone made by Whirling Wind.

Beveled mosaic inlay of sugilite stones made by Tommy Jackson.

Stampwork with two Kingman turquoise stones made by Wilson Padilla.

Courtesy of McGee's Beyond Native Tradition.

Bracelets

From top to bottom

Row 1
Diagonal lines made by Michael Tahe.

Stampwork and repoussé made by Thomas Curtis.

Stampwork, overlay, and textured background made by Thomas Curtis.

Row 2
Overlay with textured background made by Dan Jackson.

Twisted wire rope made by Thomas Curtis.

Split wire made by Alvin Thompson.

Row 3
Stampwork made by Michael Tahe.

Stampwork with beveled silver beads made by Thomas Curtis.

Stampwork made by Thomas Curtis.

Courtesy of McGee's Beyond Native Tradition.

From left to right

Stamped pot with butterflies and flowers made by Norbert Peshlakai.

Split wire bracelets made by Deborah Silversmith.

Stamped pot made by Ken Redhorse.

Stamped pot with oxblood coral stone made by Al Nez.

Left and right pair of earrings overlaid with feather, cloud, and rain designs. Center pair of earrings have lapis lazuli stones. All earrings made by Steven J. Begay.

Courtesy of Many Hands Gallery.

Watch Bracelets and Watchbands

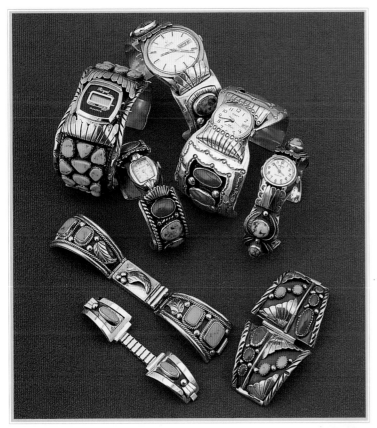

From left to right

Row 1
Stampwork with nuggets of Sleeping Beauty turquoise made by Eddie Spencer.

Stampwork with Morenci turquoise and salmon coral stones made by Roy Vandever.

Stampwork with salmon coral stones set in a shadow box. Artist unknown.

Row 2
Twisted silver rope with salmon coral and turquoise stones. Artist unknown.

Stampwork with Persian turquoise stones and appliquéd leaves. Artist unknown.

Row 3
Upper
Silver twisted rope with Blue Gem turquoise stones and appliquéd leaves. Artist unknown.

Lower
Overlay with Burnham turquoise stones and appliquéd leaves. Artist unknown.

Far right
Stampwork with turquoise and salmon coral stones with appliquéd leaves. Artist unknown.

Courtesy of Garland's Indian Jewelry.

Necklace with silver beads and pendant with mosaic and channel inlay of coral and turquoise stones with matching bracelet made by Tommy Jackson. Courtesy of The Kaibab Shop.

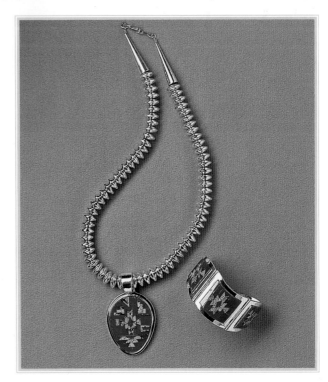

Pendant with silver overlay Flute Players with lapis lazuli and a blue topaz stone strung on lapis lazuli beads, made by Whirling Wind.

Two-sided pendant with textured cutout silver rug design with a center turquoise stone. Sides are mosaic inlay of lapis lazuli, malachite, sugilite, white shell, and turquoise. Made by Peter Nelson.

Cast pendant of bear fetish with amethyst stones strung on sugilite beads made by Whirling Wind.

Bracelet with channel silverwork with Sleeping Beauty turquoise made by Betty and Billy Betoney.

Courtesy of McGee's Beyond Native Tradition.

Sun Kachina and Eagle Kachina bola ties made with Nevada Blue turquoise and coral by Gilbert Tolino, Jr.

Courtesy of Gallup Indian Plaza.

Something Different

Fetish necklaces

Top left
Twelve buffaloes made of Picasso marble and serpentine strung on fluted silver beads.

Lower left
Nine serpentine bears strung on penn shell heishe.

Second from right
Two fish, one mole, four bears, one turtle, one gila monster, and one eagle made of serpentine and a pink shell frog. Strung on olivella shell heishe with coral.

Far right
Twelve Picasso marble buffaloes strung on fluted silver beads.

All made by Buffalo Cisco.

Courtesy of Tanner's Indian Arts.

Cluster Work

From left to right

Upper bracelet made by Eloise Kee.

All other bracelets and concha belt made by George Apachito.

Concha belt has nine conchas 2 1/2" x 2".

Stones are coral, white shell, sugilite, lapis lazuli, spiny oyster shell, black onyx, rose quartz, cat's-eye, and amethyst.

Courtesy of Gallup Indian Plaza.

Something Different

Concha belt with ten conchas 4" x 2", with seventeen petit point turquoise stones in each concha.

Necklace with 161 needlepoint turquoise stones and matching earrings with twenty-six needlepoint stones.

Bracelet with eighty-seven needlepoint turquoise stones.

All turquoise is Sleeping Beauty and all silver is overlay and channel work in a rug pattern.

Made by Betty and Billy Betoney.

Courtesy of Many Hands Gallery.

Something Different

Marbled bead necklaces made of Utah Picasso Marble, Royal Web Gemstone, turquoise, Royal Web variscite, Royal Web chalcosiderite, and serpentine.
Made by Kee Joe Benally and Danny Hoskie.
The silver beads were made by various artists.

Courtesy of Tanner's Indian Arts.

Silver stampwork and lapis lazuli beads with a silver dragonfly pendant and Royal Web Gemstone made by Kee Joe Benally and Mary Marie Yazzie

Five-strand necklace with matching earrings of Arizona peridot beads, Royal Web Gemstone, and gold beads made by Mary Marie Yazzie. The matching earrings have gold cones.

Courtesy of
Tanner's Indian Arts.

Something Different

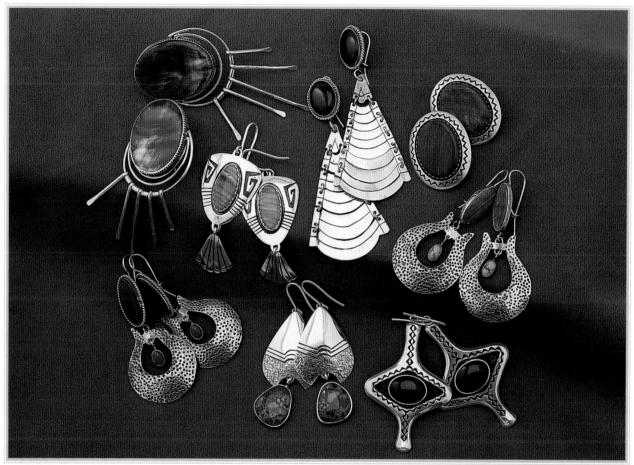

Earrings
From left to right

Row 1
Purple spiny oyster shell made by Kee Joe Benally.

Shadow box overlay and silver stampwork with orange spiny oyster shell made by Chester Kahn.

Cut silver with jade stones made by Kee Joe Benally.

Stamped shadow box silver with purple spiny oyster shell made by Chester Kahn.

Orange spiny oyster shell posts with textured stampwork and a turquoise stone dangle made by Kee Joe Benally.

Row 2
Purple spiny oyster shell posts with dangle of twisted silver rope around coral stones with dangle of textured stampwork made by Kee Joe Benally.

Textured stampwork with dangle of Damale turquoise made by Chester Kahn.

Stampwork with textured background and jade stones made by Chester Kahn.

Courtesy of Tanner's Indian Arts.

From left to right

Mosaic and channel inlay pendant with Chinese turquoise and jet made by Richard Begay. The five-strand silver square-cut beads were made by Eddie Aguilar (Santo Domingo).

Beveled, mosaic, and channel inlay pendant of Chinese turquoise set in silver incised line shadow box made by Boyd Tsosie. Strung on one-strand silver square-cut beads made by Eddie Aguilar.

Chinese turquoise pendant set in a stamped shadow box strung on silver beads made by Boyd Tsosie.

Courtesy of Many Hands Gallery.

Earrings
From left to right

Row 1

From dead pawn, round stamped concha design made with a Sleeping Beauty turquoise stone. Artist unknown. Courtesy of R. B. Burnham & Co. Trading Post.

From dead pawn, round stamped concha design made with a Sleeping Beauty turquoise stone by Harry Morgan. Courtesy of R. B. Burnham & Co. Trading Post.

From dead pawn, stamped and overlaid silver with a coral stone made by John Begay. Courtesy of R. B. Burnham & Co. Trading Post.

Row 2

Stamped oval with a Blue Gem turquoise stone made by Perry Shorty. Courtesy of the artist.

From dead pawn, stamped silver heart design with a coral stone. Artist unknown. Courtesy of R. B. Burnham & Co. Trading Post.

Twisted wire scalloped around a Morenci turquoise stone made by Perry Shorty. Courtesy of the artist.

Row 3

Twisted wire rope and silver balls and five dangles with a #8 Spider Web turquoise stone made by Perry Shorty. Courtesy of the artist.

From dead pawn, hoop earrings made with Sleeping Beauty turquoise stones. Artist unknown. Courtesy of R. B. Burnham & Co. Trading Post.

From dead pawn, appliquéd silver with two feather dangles and a King's Manassa turquoise stone. Artist unknown. Courtesy of R. B. Burnham & Co. Trading Post.

Row 4

From dead pawn, domed button shape with graduated dangles. Artist unknown. Courtesy of R. B. Burnham & Co. Trading Post.

Pins

From left to right

Row 1

Cast bear with heart-line. Artist unknown.

Stamped butterfly with a Chinese turquoise stone. Artist unknown.

Stampwork with a Chinese turquoise stone by Mary and Everett Teller.

Row 2

Appliquéd leaves with a Nevada turquoise stone. Artist unknown.

Stamped butterfly with two Nevada turquoise stones made by Larry Joe.

Repoussé and stamped silver with an Indian Mountain turquoise stone made by Edison Smith.

Row 3

Stamped concha pin with a Sleeping Beauty turquoise stone. Artist unknown.

Stamped dragonfly with a Nevada turquoise stone. Artist unknown.

Scalloped and stamped edge with dangles and a King's Manassa turquoise stone. Artist unknown.

Row 4

Overlay made by Steven Begay.

Stamped eagle made by Allison Lee.

Stampwork of Indian with copper sun. Artist unknown.

Courtesy of Garland's Indian Jewelry.

Barrettes, Hairpins and Combs

From left to right

Row 1
Barrettes
Stampwork in concha design with hawk's tails on the side and a lapis lazuli stone made by Jimmie Lee.

Stampwork with a Sleeping Beauty turquoise stone made by Jennie Blackgoat.

Repoussé and stampwork with hawk's tails on the sides made by Thomas Jim.

Row 2
Barrettes
One pair stamped in concha design. Artist unknown.

Stampwork with a Sleeping Beauty turquoise stone. Artist unknown.

Stampwork with turquoise and coral stones made by Darlene Thomas.

Row 3
Pair of hairpins stamped with a turquoise stone. Artist unknown.

Bun holder with scalloped and stamped rays made by Curtis Pete.

Pair of combs scalloped and stamped. Artist unknown.

Row 4
Pair of combs with appliqued leaves and flowers and a Nevada turquoise stone. Artist unknown.

Pair of combs with repoussé and stampwork and a Sleeping Beauty turquoise stone. Artist unknown.

Courtesy of Garland's Indian Jewelry.

From left to right

Row 1
Key holders

Stampwork with a Sleeping Beauty turquoise stone made by David Nelson.

Cast Flute Player made by Alvin Thompson.

Appliquéd leaves with a Sleeping Beauty turquoise stone made by David Nelson.

Round stamped concha design. Artist unknown.

Row 2
Money clips

Overlay rug design with a Sleeping Beauty turquoise stone made by David Nelson.

Stampwork with a Sleeping Beauty turquoise stone made by David Nelson.

Appliquéd leaves with a teardrop Sleeping Beauty turquoise stone. Artist unknown.

Row 3
Money clip and stick pins

Stampwork with double concha and butterfly design. Artist unknown.

Appliquéd leaf with turquoise stone made by Felix Tsinijinnie. Textured overlay with triangular Nevada turquoise stone made by Leo Yazzie.

Row 4
Cuff links with stampwork and carved turquoise made in 1960. Artist unknown.

Row 5
Cuff links
Stamped petal made by Thomas Jim.
Stampwork with a Nevada turquoise stone. Artist unknown.
Stamped petal made by Thomas Jim.
Courtesy of Garland's Indian Jewelry.

Cluster Work

Watchband made by Wilford Nez .
Concha belt with ten conchas (2 1/2" x 2")
made by Sam Nez.

Bracelet made in 1978 by Mary Ross.

Belt buckle (4" x 3") made by Eddie Spencer.

All turquoise
is Kingman.

Courtesy of
Gallup Indian
Plaza.

Stamped and repoussé concha belt with nine oval conchas (3 1/2") and a buckle. Each concha has a different design.

Made by Ray Tracey.

Courtesy of the artist.

Concha Belts

From left to right

*Ten conchas
(3 1/4" x 2 1/2")
with repoussé
and twisted silver
rope, with a
rectangular
Nevada Green
turquoise stone
in each concha,
made by Ned
Lee.*

*Eight conchas
(3" x 2 3/4") and
eight butterflies.
Stampwork with a
Tibetan turquoise
stone in each
concha, made by
Tim Guerro.*

*Four conchas
(4 1/4" x 3 3/4")
and five
butterflies and a
buckle (4 1/8" x
3 1/2") with
repoussé and
stampwork set on
luggage colored
leather. Center
stones are King's
Manassa
turquoise and
stones around the
edges are
malachite.
Made by Kirk
Smith.*

*Ten conchas
(2 1/2" x 2")
with a cluster of
King's Manassa
turquoise made in
1978 by Leo Nez.*

*Courtesy of
Gallup Indian
Plaza.*

Rings

From left to right

Row 1

From dead pawn, cast silver with flower and leaf appliqué and a Sleeping Beauty turquoise stone. Artist unknown. Courtesy of R. B. Burnham & Co. Trading Post.

Stamped border and bezel with a Morenci turquoise stone made by Perry Shorty. Courtesy of the artist.

From dead pawn, appliqué with one stone coral and one stone Kingman turquoise. Artist unknown. Courtesy of R. B. Burnham & Co. Trading Post.

Row 2

From dead pawn, appliqué with three-stone Kingman turquoise. Signed Duboise. Courtesy of R. B. Burnham & Co. Trading Post.

From dead pawn, appliqué with two-stone Kingman turquoise. Artist unknown. Courtesy of R. B. Burnham & Co. Trading Post.

Twisted wire border, stamped bezel, and silver balls top and bottom with a Morenci turquoise stone, made by Perry Shorty. Courtesy of the artist.

Row 3

From dead pawn, twisted wire and stamped silver balls with a Sleeping Beauty turquoise stone. Artist unknown. Courtesy of R. B. Burnham & Co. Trading Post.

From dead pawn, silver rope border with appliqué and two-stone Bisbee turquoise. Artist unknown. Courtesy of R. B. Burnham & Co. Trading Post.

Twisted wire border with three-stone Blue Gem turquoise, made by Perry Shorty. Courtesy of the artist.

14-karat gold with twisted wire border scalloped on two sides, with a natural Turquoise Mountain turquoise stone, made by Perry Shorty. Courtesy of the artist.

Rings

From left to right

Row 1

Stampwork with a Chinese turquoise stone, made by Jimmie Lee.

Twisted rope with a turquoise stone. Artist unknown.

Stampwork with a twisted rattlesnake with a turquoise head. Artist unknown.

Silver balls and appliquéd leaf with a Pilot Mountain turquoise stone. Artist unknown.

Row 2

Stampwork with a Chinese turquoise stone, made by Patrick Taylor.

Stampwork with a Kingman turquoise stone, made by Ned Nez.

Stampwork and twisted wire with two Sleeping Beauty turquoise stones. Artist unknown.

Appliquéd leaves with a Persian turquoise stone. Artist unknown.

Row 3

Stampwork with a Chinese turquoise stone, made by Patrick Taylor.

Stampwork and texturing with an oxblood coral stone, made by Leo Yazzie.

Stampwork and split wire with a Chinese turquoise stone. Artist unknown.

Cast with pink mussel shell. Artist unknown.

Row 4

Stampwork and twisted wire with a Burnham turquoise stone. Artist unknown.
Stampwork with two-stone Kingman turquoise, made by Lee Jefferson.
Stampwork and twisted wire with a Damale turquoise stone, made by M. Begay.
Stampwork with an Indian Mountain turquoise stone, made by Patrick Taylor.

Row 5

Stampwork and silver balls with a Chinese turquoise stone, made by M. Begay.
Overlay and texturing with a Chinese turquoise stone, made by Allison Lee.
Stampwork and silver balls with a Chinese turquoise stone. Artist unknown.

Courtesy of Garland's Indian Jewelry.

Rings

From left to right

Row 1
Stampwork with three coral stones, made by Chester Kahn.

Mosaic beveled mastodon ivory with a jade stone, made by Kee Joe Benally.

Textured and stampwork with a Bisbee turquoise stone. Artist unknown.

Appliqué and beveled inlay corn style with Blue Gem turquoise, made by Kee Joe Benally.

Row 2
Two stone Morenci turquoise with mosaic inlay of ivory, coral, and jet, made by Emerson Billy.

Beveled mosaic inlay with a center Persian turquoise stone, made by Kee Joe Benally.

Stampwork with Royal Web Gemstone, made by Kee Joe Benally.

Stampwork with a domed Persian turquoise stone, made by Sam Begay.

Row 3
Stampwork with three silver balls and three stone Persian turquoise, made by Chester Kahn.

Stampwork and silver balls with a coral and Bisbee turquoise stone, made by Wilson Tsosie.

Silver balls with a Bisbee turquoise stone, made by Kee Joe Benally.

Twisted rope around a coral stone, made by Ed Shirley.

Row 4
Royal Web Gemstone with coral on the sides, made by Kee Joe Benally.

Mosaic inlay of Morenci turquoise, dolomite, coral, jet, and pink shell, made by Emerson Billy.

Mosaic inlay of coral, turquoise, and jet, made by Gibson Nez .

Stampwork with mosaic inlay of turquoise and coral with center turquoise stone, made by Kee Joe Benally.

Row 5
Textured silver and mosaic inlay of Royal Web Gemstone, white shell, coral, jet, and turquoise, made by William T. Johnson.

Textured silver and stampwork with Royal Web Gemstone, made by William T. Johnson.

Appliqué with Royal Web Gemstone and coral, made by Eugene Jackson.

Textured silver and mosaic inlay of Indian Mountain turquoise, coral, dolomite, and lapis lazuli set in Arizona ironwood by Richard Tsosie.

Courtesy of Tanner's Indian Arts.

All 14-Karat Gold Bracelets

From left to right

Clockwise beginning with gold overlay story bracelet with rug weaver and hogan, made by Robert Taylor.

Overlay and mosaic inlay bracelet of Chinese turquoise, Australian opal, oxblood coral, and one diamond. The side overlay panels are the male and female Yei figures. Made by Boyd Tsosie.

Mosaic inlay and beveled stones of sugilite, salmon coral, lapis lazuli, Australian opal, and turquoise with badger paw overlaid on textured gold, made by Jesse Monongye.

Bracelet with sun face inlaid with Australian opal, salmon, angel and oxblood coral, jet, lapis lazuli, dolomite, gold lip mother-of-pearl, malachite, and turquoise, made by Jesse Monongye.

Stamped and overlay bracelet with bears and heart-line, made by Herbert Taylor.

Beveled inlay bracelet with salmon and oxblood coral, malachite, lapis lazuli, and turquoise, made by Raymond Yazzie.

Beveled inlay bracelet with oxblood coral and lapis lazuli and center stone of oxblood coral, made by Larry Joe.

Cast bracelet made by Calvin Begay. Mosaic inlay stones of lapis lazuli, Australian opal, salmon coral, sugilite, and turquoise set by Rose Ann Long.

Courtesy of Garland's Indian Jewelry.

All 14-Karat Gold Bracelets and Rings

From left to right

Link bracelets

Channel inlay with China Mountain turquoise.

Mosaic inlay with China Mountain and Sleeping Beauty turquoise, coral, opal, and jet.

Channel inlay with Sleeping Beauty turquoise, coral, opal, lapis lazuli, and jet.

From top to bottom

Rings

All channel inlay

Sleeping Beauty turquoise.

Coral.

Jet.

All made by Julian Arviso.

Courtesy of Gallup Indian Plaza.

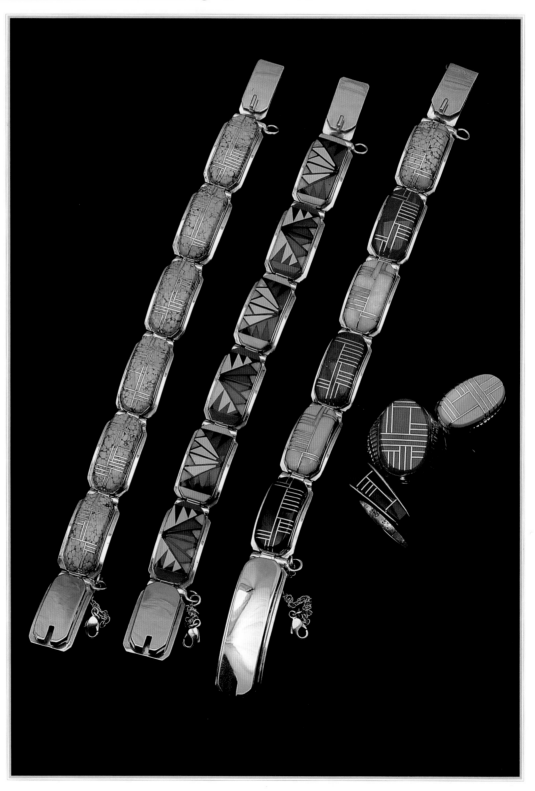

All 14-Karat Gold

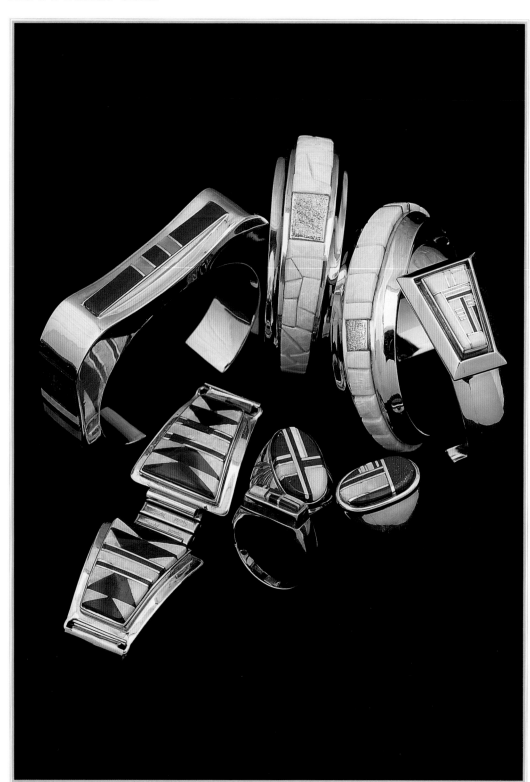

From left to right

Row 1
*Channel inlay of
sugilite and opal.*

*Beveled mosaic
inlay with opal
and brushed gold.*

*Beveled mosaic
inlay with opal
and brushed gold.*

*Channel inlay of
sugilite and opal.*

Row 2
*Mosaic and
channel inlay
watchband with
sugilite, opal,
and coral.*

*Two oval rings of
channel inlay
with opal and
lapis lazuli.*

*Rectangular ring
of channel inlay
with opal and
sugilite.*

*All made by Julian
Arviso.*

*Courtesy of Gallup
Indian Plaza.*

All 14-Karat Gold Earrings

From left to right

Row 1
Appliquéd with turquoise and oxblood coral, made by Oliver Smith.

Tufa cast with oxblood coral cabochons made by Al Nez.

Turquoise channel work set by Rose Ann Long and gold work made by Rick Tolino.

Row 2
Inlay of lapis lazuli and turquoise by Wilbert Muskett, Jr. and gold work made by Rick Tolino.

Angel and oxblood coral and Australian opal made by Vernon Hoskie.

Three gold dangles. Artist unknown.

Row 3
Stamped and fluted beads. Artist unknown.

Stamped and appliquéd Eagle Dancer with black onyx made by Richard Long.

Appliquéd with Australian opal made by Oliver Smith.

Courtesy of Garland's Indian Jewelry.

All 14-Karat Gold Earrings

From top to bottom

Row 1

Channel and mosaic inlay of turquoise, sugilite, and Australian opal. Artist unknown.

Stamped edge with a turquoise stone. Artist unknown.

Channel inlay with lapis lazuli and Australian opal. Artist unknown.

Twisted rope edge with an oxblood coral stone made by Loren Bahé.

Row 2

Paiute turquoise with three balls. Artist unknown.

Green Nevada turquoise with three balls. Artist unknown.

Turquoise channel inlay. Artist unknown.

Courtesy of Garland's Indian Jewelry.

All 14-Karat Gold

From left to right

Channel inlay coral and opal bracelet.

Mosaic inlay reversible pendant of bear and sun face made with white shell, coral, sugilite, and turquoise strung on an eight-strand coral necklace.

Channel inlay coral watch tips.

Channel inlay opal and coral ring.

Channel inlay coral link bracelet.

All made by Julian Arviso.

Courtesy of Gallup Indian Plaza.

All 14-Karat Gold
All Channel and Mosaic Inlay

Choker with four diamonds.

Pendant inlaid with Afghanistan lapis lazuli, *Australian opal, and seven diamonds, pavé technique.

Matching bracelet with thirteen diamonds, pavé technique.

Made by Ray Tracey.
Courtesy of the artist.

*Pavé technique. A setting in which jewels are placed close together so as to show no metal.

All 14-Karat Gold

Necklace with oxblood coral, lapis lazuli, turquoise, and gold beads.

Reversible pendant with Corn Maiden Kachina on one side, made with ironwood, salmon coral, gold lip mother-of-pearl, jet, turquoise, and dolomite. Reverse side of pendant is of Monument Valley galaxy made with sugilite, Australian opal, lapis lazuli, salmon, angel and oxblood coral, dolomite, and malachite. This won First Prize, Best in Category, and Best in Class at the Gallup Inter-Tribal Indian Ceremonial in Gallup, New Mexico in 1993.

Beveled inlay bracelet with Australian opal, turquoise, sugilite, salmon, angel and oxblood coral, and lapis lazuli.

Mosaic inlay ring made with oxblood coral, dolomite, turquoise, gold lip mother-of-pearl, and lapis lazuli.

All made by Jesse Monongye.

Courtesy of Garland's Indian Jewelry.

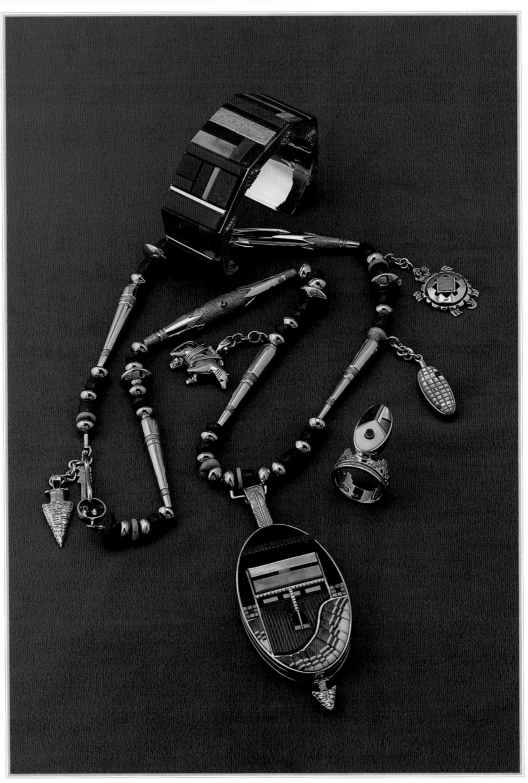

All 14-Karat Gold

From top to bottom

Row 1
Cast gold bracelet with a Lone Mountain Spider Web turquoise stone, made by Della and Francis James.

Gold reversible brooch/pendant with filigree wire work and a Chinese Spider Web turquoise stone, made by Perry Shorty.

Row 2
Textured gold on silver ring with a Bisbee turquoise stone, made by Kee Joe Benally.

Gold ring with scalloped bezel work and a Lone Mountain Spider Web turquoise stone, made by Sam Begay.

Textured gold earrings entitled, "It's the Wind", with a Persian turquoise stone, made by Kee Joe Benally.

Row 3
Cast and stamped bola tie with Dontso figure* and a Persian turquoise stone, made by Chester Kahn.

Courtesy of Tanner's Indian Arts.

*Water figure

All 14-Karat Gold

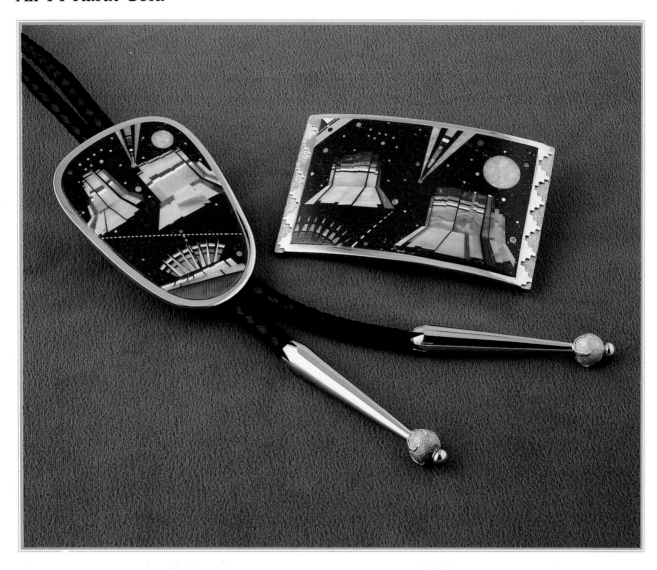

Mosaic inlay bola tie and belt buckle with lapis lazuli, Australian opal, dolomite, malachite, salmon, angel and oxblood coral, white mother-of-pearl, and turquoise.

The reverse side of the bola tie and belt buckle (3 1/2" x 2 1/4") has an overlaid eagle.

Both made by Jesse Monongye.

They depict the evening sky in Monument Valley.

The dotted lines represent Highway 66.

Courtesy of Garland's Indian Jewelry.

All 14-Karat Gold

From left to right

Overlay and textured gold on silver watchband with Flute Players made by Robert Taylor.

Overlay and textured gold rings (2 bands) with Flute Players made by Robert Taylor.

Gold on silver ring (band) with maze design made by Robert Taylor.

Overlay and stamped gold ring with flower design made by Howard Nelson.

Overlay and textured gold bracelet with Flute Players made by Robert Taylor.

Courtesy of McGee's Beyond Native Tradition.

All 14-Karat Gold

Gold overlay on textured silver earrings and pendant of bear made by Jack Tom.

Gold ring, watchbands, and pendant are mosaic and channel inlay of opal. The pendant has black onyx with a beveled opal stone. All made by Fannie Bitsoi and Phil Russell.

Courtesy of McGee's Beyond Native Tradition.

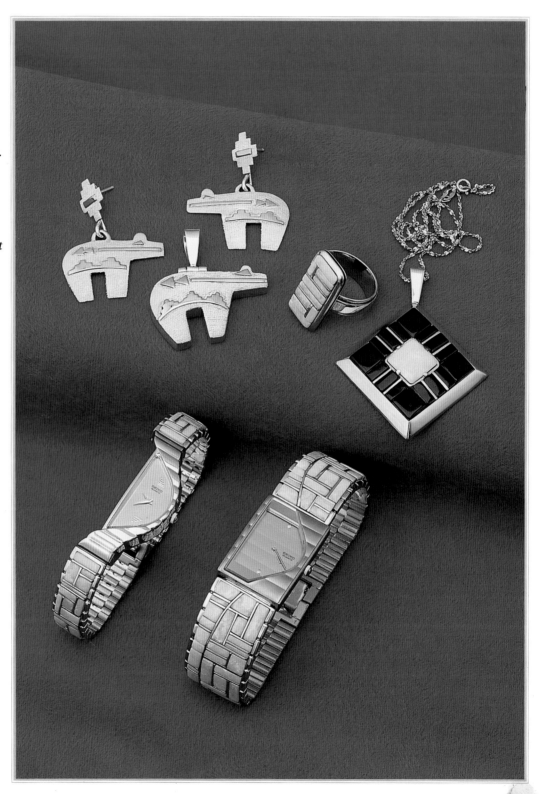

Rings

From left to right

Row 1

14-karat gold ring inlaid with sugilite, dolomite, turquoise, oxblood coral, and spiny oyster shell, made by Jesse Monongye.

Sterling silver ring inlaid with sugilite, turquoise, oxblood coral, and lapis lazuli. Coral stone is set in 14-karat gold. Made by Jesse Monongye.

Sterling silver ring inlaid with malachite, dolomite, lapis lazuli, sugilite, oxblood coral, and turquoise. Sun face is set in 14-karat gold. Made by Jesse Monongye.

Row 2

Sterling silver ring inlaid with oxblood coral, lapis lazuli, gold lip mother-of-pearl, and turquoise. Round turquoise stone is set in 14-karat gold. Made by Jesse Monongye.

14-karat gold ring with turquoise, jet, sugilite, oxblood coral, and opal creating a female Yei figure. Made by Norton Becenti.

14-karat gold ring with mosaic and channel inlay of turquoise, lapis lazuli, and gold inlay creating a face. Made by Norton Becenti.

Row 3

14-karat gold ring inlaid with oxblood coral, sugilite, lapis lazuli, turquoise, Australian opal, and gold circles, made by Boyd Tsosie.

14-karat gold ring inlaid with turquoise, sugilite, oxblood coral, and lapis lazuli with gold dots, leaves, and floral appliqué, made by Boyd Tsosie.

14-karat gold ring inlaid with beveled turquoise, angel and oxblood coral, Australian opal, malachite, sugilite, and gold channels, made by Raymond Yazzie.

14-karat gold ring inlaid with beveled sugilite, lapis lazuli, Australian opal, gold channels, leaves, and floral appliqué, made by Boyd Tsosie.

Courtesy of Garland's Indian Jewelry.

Cast silver bracelet and ring with Yei figure using a micro-fine mosaic inlay technique with turquoise, lapis lazuli, jet, red and pink coral, white shell, and lavulite, made by Irene and Carl Clark.

Gold bracelet and ring of channel inlay with lapis lazuli and red and pink coral, made by Julian Arviso.

Courtesy of Gallup Indian Plaza.

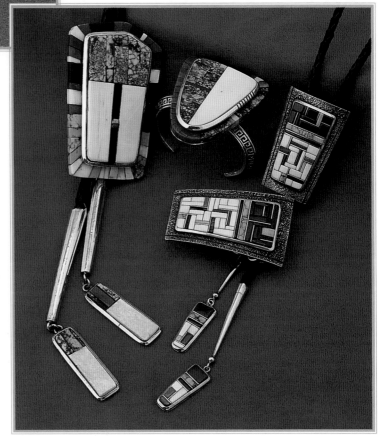

On left

Bola tie (3 3/4" x 2 1/2") with matching tips and matching bracelet inlaid with turquoise, jet, dolomite, and oxblood coral. The silver on the bracelet is overlaid with Greek key design.

On right
Bola tie with matching tips and matching belt buckle (2 3/4" x 1 3/4") has textured silver and beveled mosaic channel inlay of turquoise, malachite, pink and red coral, dolomite, sugilite, and opal.

All made by Fannie Bitsoi and Phil Russell.

Courtesy of Many Hands Gallery.

Bola Ties and Belt Buckles

Overlay and stamped textured silver belt buckle and bola tie set with Bisbee turquoise, made by Lee A. Yazzie.

Courtesy of Tanner's Indian Arts.

From left to right

Bola tie with silver shadow box and silver overlay with center turquoise stone. Lower half is beveled and inlaid with turquoise, oxblood coral, and malachite.

Matching belt buckle (2 3/4" x 2") with silver shadow box of an eagle. Beveled inlay with dolomite, oxblood coral, and turquoise.
Both made by Richard Tsosie.

Tufa cast bola tie of two lizards and an inlaid turtle of oxblood and salmon coral, lapis lazuli, and turquoise.

Matching tufa cast belt buckle (3" x 2"), inlaid with lapis lazuli and oxblood coral with faces of two Yei figures.
Both made by Ric Charlie.

Bola tie, overlay and stampwork with two Apache Mountain Spirit Dancers and hawk's tails at each side.

Matching belt buckle (3" x 2 1/4"), stampwork and overlay. Both made by Curtis Pete.

Courtesy of Garland's Indian Jewelry.

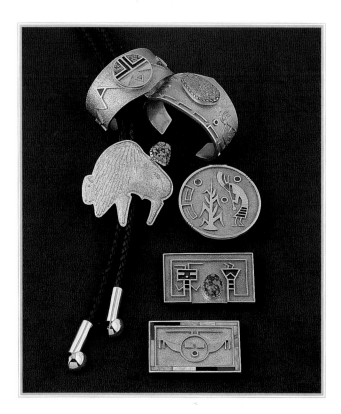

All Tufa Cast

From left to right

Bola tie with buffalo and turquoise stone.

Bracelet with sun face and lightning inlaid with Chinese turquoise, angel and oxblood coral.

Bracelet with a Chinese turquoise stone with Flute Player, petroglyphic designs, circles, and deer tracks inlaid with oxblood coral.

Round belt buckle, 2 1/2" in diameter, with Flute Player and corn inlaid with oxblood and salmon coral, and turquoise.

Belt buckle (2 1/2" x 1 1/2") with a Chinese turquoise stone and a Rainbow Yei figure.

Belt buckle (2 1/2" x 1 1/2") with a sandpainting sun inlaid with jet, white agate, turquoise, and angel and oxblood coral.

All made by Jason Begay.

Courtesy of Garland's Indian Jewelry.

From top to bottom

Row 1
Ring with five-stone Chinese turquoise. Artist unknown.

Ring with five-stone turquoise made by M.R.N.

Row 2
Bola tie with six-stone, Chinese turquoise made by Wilson Padilla.

Row 3
Bracelet with twisted rope, stampwork, and appliquéd silver leaf with six-stone Kingman turquoise, made by Tom Bahe.

Stamped belt buckle with one-stone turquoise, made by Norman Bia.

Ring with three-stone Chinese turquoise. Artist unknown.

Stamped earrings made with a Chinese turquoise stone by Ramona.

Courtesy of McGee's Beyond Native Tradition.

Bola Ties

From left to right

Silver overlay and stampwork with a black onyx stone, made by Kee Nez.

Textured and stamped silver and mosaic inlay stones consisting of turquoise, opal, lapis lazuli, malachite, sugilite, and dolomite, made by Peter Nelson.

Stampwork with a Kingman turquoise stone set in a shadow box, made by Thomas Nez.

Stamped bola tie and belt buckle set with stones of black onyx, made by Howard Nelson.

Courtesy of McGee's Beyond Native Tradition.

Bola Ties

From left to right

Stamp and repoussé work. Artist unknown.

Traditional Navajo stampwork in a concha design with shadow box around a Chinese turquoise stone. Artist unknown.

Stampwork with a Blue Gem turquoise stone made by Carson Blackgoat.

Stampwork made by Ron Bedoni.

Stampwork with a Chinese Spider Web turquoise stone made by Kee Joe Benally.

Stampwork with a Blue Gem turquoise stone made by Carson Blackgoat.

Courtesy of Tanner's Indian Arts.

Overlay silver bracelets, bola ties, and belt buckle (3 1/2" x 2 1/4") in rug pattern and feather designs, made by Steven J. Begay.

Courtesy of Many Hands Gallery.

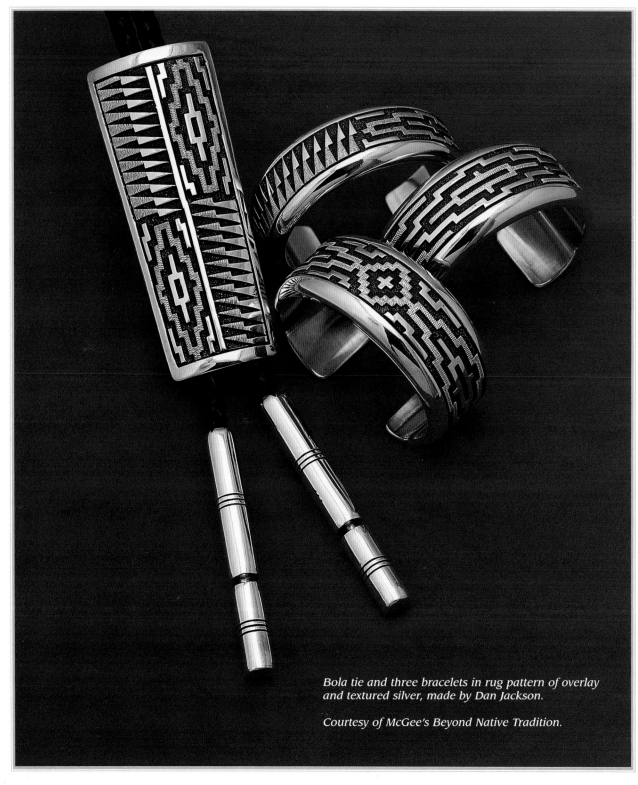

Bola tie and three bracelets in rug pattern of overlay and textured silver, made by Dan Jackson.

Courtesy of McGee's Beyond Native Tradition.

Belt Buckles

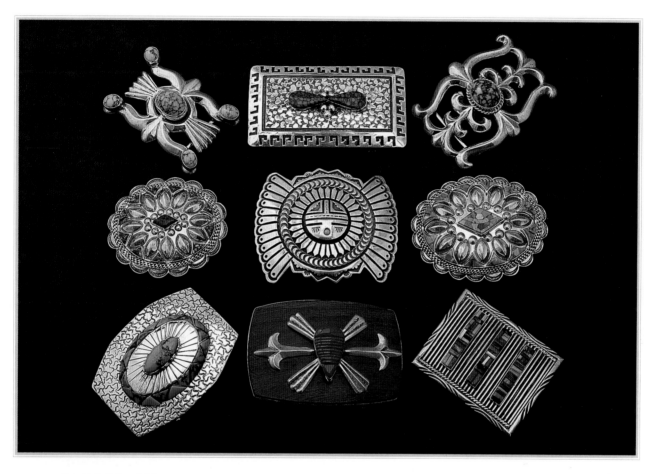

From left to right

Row 1

Cast silver with five Persian turquoise stones made by Betty Rose Billie.

Hammered center with overlay border and two Persian turquoise stones made by Kee Joe Benally.

Cast silver with one Persian turquoise stone made by Wilbur Anderson.

Row 2

Stamp and repoussé work with Royal Web Gemstone on edges and a lapis lazuli stone in the center made by William T. Johnson.

Stampwork with sun face and a Persian turquoise stone made by Emerson Bill.

Stamp and repoussé work with mosaic Blue Gem turquoise, lapis lazuli, and coral stone. Artist unknown.

Row 3

Stampwork and textured silver with circle of triangular cut Bisbee turquoise stones and an oval Bisbee turquoise stone, made by Kee Joe Benally.

Ironwood on silver with a silver cast decoration and a beveled mosaic coral stone, made by Kee Joe Benally.

Channeled silver with beveled mosaic pattern of coral, turquoise, lapis lazuli, ironwood, and white shell made by Donny Clark.

Courtesy of Tanner's Indian Arts.

Ranger Belt Buckles

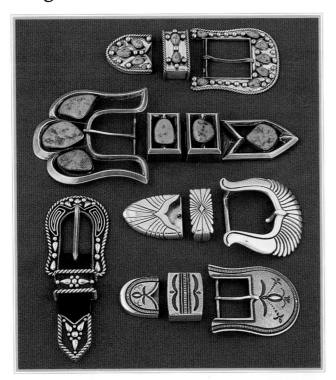

Three piece set with twelve Sleeping Beauty turquoise teardrop stones made by Betty and Billy Betoney.

Four piece cast set with six Blue Gem turquoise stones. Artist unknown.

On left, with appliquéd and twisted silver rope made by Betty and Billy Betoney.

Three piece set with stamped silver made by Thomas Curtis.

Three piece set stamped with flower design, made by Patrick Taylor.

Courtesy of Garland's Indian Jewelry.

Row 1
From top to bottom

Stamped bracelet with a Sleeping Beauty turquoise stone set in a shadow box made by Dan Jackson.

Overlay with textured background belt buckle with a Darling Darlene turquoise stone, made by Howard Nelson.

Row 2
Overlay and textured bola tie and belt buckle set, each having a Morenci turquoise stone made by Howard Nelson.

Row 3
Open-channeled graduated link bracelet made by Whirling Wind.

Courtesy of McGee's Beyond Native Tradition

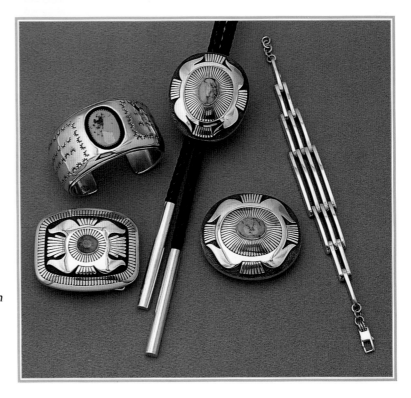

Repoussé and stamped silver bracelet with concha design.

Repoussé and stamped silver ketoh with hawk's tails on the side and six dimes on each side dating from 1926-1945.

Repoussé and stamped silver bola tie.

Repoussé and stamped silver concha belt with fifteen conchas.

Stampwork ranger belt buckle on leather belt.

All made by Thomas Curtis.

Courtesy of McGee's Beyond Native Tradition.

Variation of a squash blossom necklace with matching earrings with overlay and textured background, with eleven coral stones, made by David Lincoln.

Bracelet with nine oval coral stones, made by Howard Nelson.

Belt buckle and bola tie set with stamped and textured background, each having one coral stone, made by C. J.

Ring with beveled, mosaic, and channel inlay of coral, turquoise, black onyx, malachite, and sugilite, made by Fannie Bitsoi and Phil Russell.

Courtesy of McGee's Beyond Native Tradition.

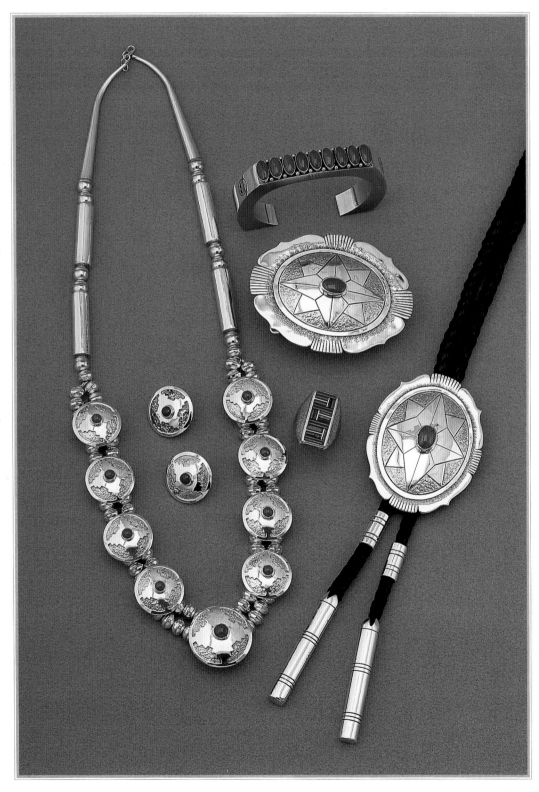

All jewelry is made of Royal Web Gemstone, and the loose pieces depict the different colors and patterns that come from the Royal Web Gemstone mine.

Stampwork and textured silver necklace made by Chester Kahn.

Bracelet on left has a twisted square wire and stamped wings along a rectangular stone, made by John Benally, Jr.

Bracelet on right has overlay and stampwork made by Chester Kahn.

Textured earrings with stampwork made by Kee Joe Benally.

Courtesy of Tanner's Indian Arts.

Belt buckle, bola tie, and bracelet have stampwork and appliqué with Morenci turquoise stones.

The squash blossom necklace is made with Morenci turquoise.

All made by Leon Garcia.

Courtesy of Gallup Indian Plaza.

From left to right

Overlay and stamped disk and barrel bead necklace with a pendant of oxblood coral stone made by Howard Nelson.

Overlay and stamped squash blossom necklace with matching earrings made by Steven Begay.

Courtesy of Garland's Indian Jewelry.

Variation of a squash blossom necklace with Liberty coins ranging in age from 1919-1935. Globe turquoise is on the cast naja.

Squash blossom necklace with 109 Blue Gem turquoise stones with cast corn.

Both made by Perry Shorty.

Courtesy of the artist.

Matched set of hinged bracelet, necklace, and earrings.

The silver work was made by Norton Becenti.

The channel work and mosaic inlay stones of spiny oyster shell, lapis lazuli, turquoise, sugilite, and dolomite were set by Rick Tolino.

Courtesy of Garland's Indian Jewelry.

Necklace and
matching earrings
inlaid with lapis
lazuli, gold lip
mother-of-pearl,
sugilite, dolomite,
turquoise, and
oxblood coral.
Silver work was
made by Calvin
Begay and the
stones were set by
Wilbert Muskett, Jr.

Courtesy of
Garland's
Indian Jewelry.

Stamped and repoussé bracelet made by Edison Smith.

Stamped cornflower necklace and matching earrings made by Thomas Jim.

The necklace won the Squash Blossom of Colorado Award at the Southwestern Association of Indian Affairs 1989 Annual Indian Market in Sante Fe, New Mexico. This award is for excellence in design and execution of a squash blossom necklace.

Courtesy of Garland's Indian Jewelry.

*Variation of a
squash blossom
necklace with
silver stampwork
and triangular
Chinese turquoise
stones strung
with fluted silver
and turquoise
beads with
matching
earrings, made by
Chester Kahn.*

*Courtesy of
Tanner's Indian
Arts.*

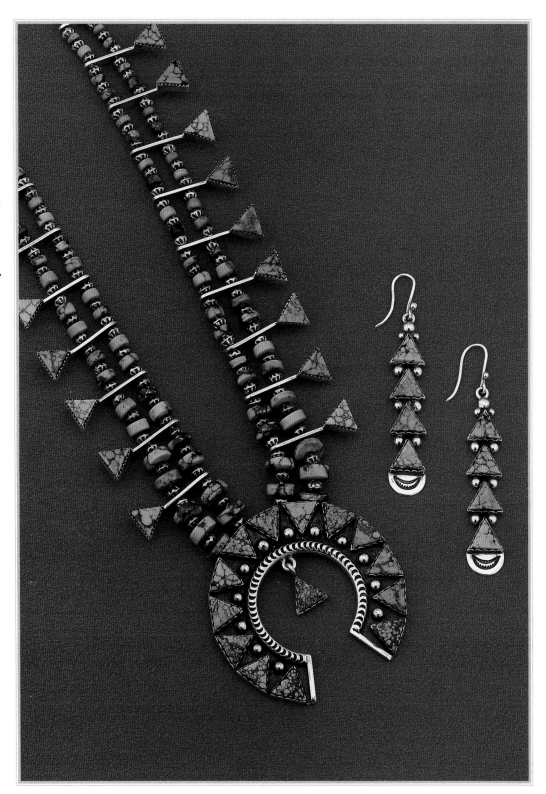

The Author

Backpacking and river-running exploits led Theda Bassman into Arizona and New Mexico, where she met the Native Americans. Their feelings for nature and the environment were so similar to hers that she developed many friendships with them in a short time. For the past fifty years she has traveled to the Indian reservations, not only to visit her friends, but also to buy their crafts. In 1972, she opened a gallery in Beverly Hills, California, called "The Indian and I." When she and her husband retired, they moved to Palm Desert, California, where they now live. They also have a cabin on the Mogollon Rim in Northern Arizona, where they spend their time in the forest and traveling to the nearby Indian reservations. Theda has judged Indian shows at the Museum of Northern Arizona in Flagstaff, Arizona, the Inter-Tribal Indian Ceremonial in Gallup, New Mexico, the Santa Fe Indian Market in Santa Fe, New Mexico, the O'Odham Tash in Casa Grande, Arizona. And the American Indian and Western Relic Show in Pasadena, California. Theda Bassman is a feminist, an environmentalist, and a lover of chamber music. She is a member of Greenpeace, the Sierra Club, the Hemlock Society, and is a Hospice volunteer. *The Beauty of Navajo Jewelry* is her eighth book.

Other Books by Theda Bassman

Hopi Kachina Dolls and Their CarversI
The Kachina Dolls of Cecil Calnimptewa Their Power Their Splendor
The Beauty of Hopi Jewelry
Zuni Jewelry (co-authored with Michael Bassman)
Treasures of the Zuni
Treasures of the Hopi
Treasures of the Navajo

The Photographer

Gene Balzer is a Professor of Photography at the University of Northern Arizona in Flagstaff, Arizona. He has photographed most of the collection of the Museum of Northern Arizona, and conducts field trips to various archaeological sites and national parks on the Colorado Plateau. Balzer's photographs have appeared in *Arizona Highways, American Indian Art Magazine, Southwest Profile, Plateau Magazine, The World and I,* and *The Indian Country Guide.* One of his photographs was featured on the cover of a compact disk by Native American flutist R. Carlos Nakai. Balzer is the photographer for all of Theda Bassman's books.

Index of Artists

A
Abeita, Jefferson,21
Aguilar, Eddie (Santo Domingo) 30
Anderson, Evelyn,14
Anderson, Wilbur,61
Apachito, George, 26
Arviso, Julian,20,42,43,46,54

B
Bahé, Loren,45
Bahe, Tom,56
Becenti, Norton,19,20,53,69
Bedoni, Ron,58
Begay, Calvin,19,41,70
Begay, Jason,56
Begay, John,31
Begay, M.,39
Begay, Richard,30
Begay, Sam,14,40,49
Begay, Steven J.,22,32,59,67
Benally, John, Jr.,65
Benally, Kee Joe,18,28,29,40,49,58,61,65
Betoney, Betty,24,27,62
Betoney, Billy ,24,27,62
Bia, Norman ,56
Bill, Emerson,61
Billie, Betty Rose,61
Billy, Emerson,40
Bitsoi, Fannie,52,54,64
Blackgoat, Carson,58
Blackgoat, Jennie,33

C
Charlie, Ric,55
Cisco, Buffalo,26
C. J.,64
Clark, Carl,54
Clark, Donny,61
Clark, Irene,54
Curtis, Thomas,22,62,63

D
Duboise,38

G
Garcia, Leon,66
Guerro, Tim,37

H
Harrison, Jim,19
Hoskie, Danny,28
Hoskie, Vernon,44

J
Jackson, Dan,21,22,60,62
Jackson, Eugene,40
Jackson, Tommy,Title Page,21,23
James, Della,15,17,18,49
James, Francis,15,17,18,49
Jasper, John,20
Jefferson, Lee,39
Jim, Thomas,33,34,71
Joe, Larry,32,41
Joe, Zora,20
Johnson, William T.,40,61

K
Kahn, Chester,29,40,49,69,72
Kee, Eloise,26
Kee, Irene ,20

L
Lee, Allison,32,39
Lee, Jimmie,33,39
Lee, Ned,37
Lincoln, David,64
Livingston, Gloria,20
Livingston, Jake (Navajo/ Zuni),Dedication Page,,8,9
Long, Charles Chee,13,18
Long, Richard,44
Long, Rose Ann,20,41,44

M
Monongye, Jesse,19,41,48,50,53
Morgan, Harry,31
M. R. N.,56
Muskett, Wilbert, Jr.,20,44,70

Index of Artists

N

Nelson, David,34
Nelson, Howard,51,57,62,64,67
Nelson, Peter,24,33,57
Nez, Al,22,44
Nez, Gibson,19,40
Nez, James,19
Nez, Kee,57
Nez, Leo,37
Nez, Ned,39
Nez, Sam,35
Nez, Thomas,57
Nez, Wilford ,35

P

Padilla, Wilson,21,56
Panteah, Clayton (Zuni),19
Peshlakai, Norbert,22
Pete, Curtis,35,55
Porter, Minnie,15

R

Ramona,56
Redhorse, Ken,22
Ross, Mary,35
Russell, Phil,52,54,64

S

Shirley, Ed,14,40
Shorty, Perry,8,9,31,38,49,68
Silversmith, Deborah,22
Smith, Edison,32,71
Smith, Kirk,37
Smith, Oliver,44
Spencer, Eddie,23,35

T

Tahe, Michael,22
Taylor, Herbert,41
Taylor, Patrick,39,62
Taylor, Robert,41,51
Teller, Everett,32
Teller, Mary,32

Thomas, Darlene,33
Thompson, Alvin,22,34
Tolino, Gilbert, Jr. ,25
Tolino, Rick ,20,44,69
Tom, Jack,52
Tracey, Ray,Front Cover,36,47
Tsinijinnie, Felix,34
Tsosie, Boyd,19,30,41,53,Back Cover
Tsosie, Richard,40,55
Tsosie, Wilson,40

V

Vandever, Roy,23

W

Whirling Wind,21,24,62

Y

Yazzie, Cecilia,21
Yazzie, Joe,14
Yazzie, Lee A.,14,55
Yazzie, Leo,34,39
Yazzie, Mary Marie,28
Yazzie, Raymond,8,19,41,53
Yellowhorse, Steve,16

Glossary

Appliqué: A design cut out of one piece of silver or gold and soldered onto another piece.

Beveled: A stone cut on a slant.

Bezel: A thin strip of silver around a stone that is soldered to the silver base.

Bow Guard: see Ketoh

Cabochon: A stone that is cut flat on the bottom with a rounded top.

Channel inlay: A design of shell or stone set with a bezel between each stone. The stones are sanded level and polished.

Cluster: A group of tear-drop or round stones that are individually set.

Dontso figure: A water figure.

Filigree: A lacelike fine silver or gold wire applied to another silver or gold surface.

Fluted beads: Having a ridged line radiating from the center to the soldered edge of each half.

Gato: see Ketoh

Hogan: A dwelling place of the Navajo.

Ketoh: Sometimes called bow guard or gato. A leather guard that protects the wrist from the snap of the bowstring. Now worn by the men in ceremonial dances.

Mosaic inlay: Patterns or designs using small pieces of stones that are not separated by silver.

Naja: A crescent-shaped pendant, often hanging from a squash blossom necklace.

Needlepoint: Stones that are shaped to a fine point at each end and set in a silver or gold bezel.

Overlay: A design is cut out of one piece of silver and soldered onto a plain piece of silver and then the design is oxidized with liver of sulfate. Also, some overlay is made by soldering a gold design onto the silver.

Pavé technique: A setting in which jewels are placed close together so as to show no metal.

Petit point: An oval stone ground to a fine point at one end, rounded on the other end and set in a bezel.

Petroglyph: A prehistoric rock carving.

Repoussé: A design that is formed in relief by hammering from the underside.

Sand Cast: The process of casting made in a mold of sand, then melted silver or gold is poured into the mold. A prototype mold is designed so that many pieces of jewelry may be produced.

Stampwork: The use of a tool with the design on one end and hammered until the design is impressed into the silver or gold.

Tufa Cast: A design is carved onto one side of a mold, and another plain piece of tufa, which is of volcanic origin, is tightly joined to the carved side, and then melted silver or gold is poured into the mold. When it has cooled, the metal is removed and then filed and polished. Usually only one piece of jewelry is achieved per cast, and then the mold is destroyed.

Yei figure: The holy people of the Navajo.

Yei-bi-chai: The persons who portray the Yeis in the Navajo sacred dances.

Suggested Reading

Adair, John
1944   *The Navajo & Pueblo Silversmiths*. Norman, University of Oklahoma Press.

Ashton, Robert and Sharon
1975   Southwest Indian Silverwork, *Ray Manley's Southwestern Indian Arts & Crafts*. Tucson, Arizona, Ray Manley Photography, Inc.

1976   Jewelry, *Arizona Highways Indian Arts and Crafts*. Phoenix, Arizona Highways.

Babbitt, James E.
1986   Trading Posts Along the Little Colorado River, *Plateau Magazine*, Volume 57, No 3. Flagstaff, Museum of Northern Arizona.

Bedinger, Margery
1973   *Indian Silver: Navajo and Pueblo Jewelers*. Albuquerque, University of New Mexico Press.

Bennett, Edna Mae and John F.
1973   *Turquoise Jewelry of the Indian of the Southwest*. Colorado Springs, Colorado, Turquoise Books.

Blue, Martha
1986   A Navajo Ken of Traders and Trading Posts, *Plateau Magazine*, Volume 57, No 3. Flagstaff, Museum of Northern Arizona.

Brundige-Baker, Joan
1986   Restoration and Preservation of Historic Trading Posts, *Plateau Magazine*, Volume 57, No 3. Flagstaff, Museum of Northern Arizona.

Cirillo, Dexter
1992   *Southwestern Indian Jewelry*. New York, Abbeville Press.

Clark, Jackson
1987   Jake Livingston: IACA's 1988 "Artist of the Year," *The Indian Trader Newspaper*, November, 1987, Gallup, New Mexico.

Eaton, Linda B.
1993   *Native American Art of the Southwest*. Lincolnwood, Illinois, Publications International Ltd.

Eddington, Patrick and Susan Makov
1995   *Trading Post Guidebook*. Flagstaff, Arizona, Northland Publishing.

Ellsberg, Helen
1977   Ketohs, *American Indian Art Magazine*, Summer, 1977. Scottsdale, Arizona.

Ferguson, Erna
1931   *Dancing Gods: Indian Ceremonials of New Mexico and Arizona*. Albuquerque, University of New Mexico Press.

Frank, Larry and Millard J. Holbrook II
1990   *Indian Silver Jewelry of the Southwest*. West Chester, Pennsylvania, Schiffer Publishing, Ltd.

Furst, Peter T. and Jill L.
1982   *North American Indian Art*. New York, Rizzoli International Publications, Inc.

Gilpin, Laura
1968   *The Enduring Navajo*. Austin, University of Texas Press.

Hait, Pam
1979   Gold, Silver and a Touch of Forever, *Arizona Highways Magazine*, April, 1979. Phoenix, Arizona Highways.

Hammons, Lee and Gertrude Frances Hill
1975   *Turquoise and the Navajo*. Glendale, Arizona, Arizona Maps and Books.

Suggested Reading

Jacka, Lois Essary and Jerry
1994   *Enduring Traditions*. Flagstaff, Arizona, Northland Publishing.

1995   *Navajo Jewelry*. Flagstaff, Arizona, Northland Publishing.

Liverino, Basilio
1975   Coral—"Red Gold" of Indian Jewelry, *Arizona Highways Magazine*, March, 1975. Phoenix, Arizona Highways.

Mercurio, Gian and Maxymilian L. Peschel
1994   *The Guide to Trading Posts and Pueblo*s. Cortez, Colorado, Lonewolf Publishing.

Neumann, David L.
1974   Turquoise and Indian Jewelry, *Arizona Highways Magazine,* January, 1974, Phoenix, Arizona Highways.

Neumann, David L. and Robert and Sharon Ashton
1976   Jewelry, *Arizona Highways Indian Arts and Crafts*. Phoenix, Arizona Highways.

Page, Susanne and Jake
1995   *Navajo*. New York, Harry N. Abrams, Inc.

Pogue, Joseph E.
1915   *Turquoise*. Glorieta, New Mexico, The Rio Grande Press Inc.

Stacey, Joseph
1975   OLD PAWN...the <u>real</u>, real Indian Jewelry, *Arizona Highways Magazine*, March, 1975. Phoenix, Arizona Highways.

1974   The Arizona Highways Hall of Fame Classics, *Arizona Highways Magazine*, August, 1974. Phoenix, Arizona Highways.

Tanner, Clara Lee
1968   *Southwest Indian Craft Arts*. Tucson, University of Arizona Press.

Tanner, Clara Lee and Joe Ben Wheat
1975   *Ray Manley's Portraits & Turquoise of Southwest Indians*. Tucson, Arizona, Ray Manley Photography, Inc.

Turnbaugh, William A. and Sarah Peabody Turnbaugh
1988   *Indian Jewelry of the American Southwest*. West Chester, Pennsylvania, Schiffer Publishing, Ltd.

Waters, Frank
1970   *Masked Gods*. New York, Ballantine Books.

Woodward, Arthur
1971   *Navajo Silver*. Flagstaff, Arizona, Northland Press.

Wright, Barton
1989   *Hallmarks of the Southwest*. West Chester, Pennsylvania, Schiffer Publishing, Ltd.

Back Cover Photo

All 14-karat gold

Link bracelet of oxblood coral, sugilite, and turquoise. The two gold side pieces are overlaid Yei-bi-chai figures.

Necklace and matching earrings are of oxblood coral, Australian opal, sugilite, lapis lazuli, and turquoise.

Overlay and mosaic inlay ring is of oxblood coral, sugilite, Australian opal, lapis lazuli, and two diamonds.

All made by Boyd Tsosie.

Private collection.